WHAT PEOPLE ARE SAYING ABOUT
STOP BEING THE STRING ALONG:
A RELATIONSHIP GUIDE TO BEING ⌐   Ḙ

*"Stop Being the String Along i*ᶜ
to create a joyful, fully cᶜ
tical, *empowering* guidε
shows you how to stop '   ᵣela-
tionship that reflects the tᵤ   ᵣates your
joy, and heals you—and yoᵤ   ᵤ process."

—Julia Rogers Hamrick,   ⌐ᵤor of *Recreating Eden*

"This book by Barbara Rose is the ultimate spiritual guide
to healing yourself to attract your ultimate relationship. Not
reading this book means you are not willing to be in a
happy, balanced relationship."

—Philippe Matthews, author,
www.SHOCKphilosophy.com;
host of The Philippe Matthews Show

"This is a wonderful and poignant book on the essence of
what makes a relationship truly work and how to heal relationships that are on a downward spiral. As a translator, I
look deep inside a book into the mind of the writer so I can
understand enough of the subject to relay it in a different
language. From that perspective, this book gives excellent
advice, full of wisdom, and presented very clearly."

— Jaime Minino, Mincor Spanish Language Translation
Company

"Is there something missing from your relationship? If the
answer is yes, then this book is a must for you! Barbara Rose
has a unique gift that few authors possess. She reaches to the
core of her being and dives deep within her own heart to
answer the most difficult questions facing relationships at
this time, and she gives answers that all souls have searched
for since the beginning of time. God, what does it take to
experience true unconditional love in my everyday relationships with myself and others? How can I empower myself to

be authentic and to be who I am truly meant to be? What does it take to make life work? Read on folks, the answers are here at last! Once this awareness is embraced, you become 'The One.'"

—Dennis Holmes, Sol Prophet

"Barbara has embraced a subject that we have all struggle with. Please read *Stop Being the String Along: A Relationship Guide to Being THE ONE*. It is a wake-up call for all who find themselves entangled in their own inner fears of being loved for who they are. This book will touch those who find that they change their personal demeanor to be accepted or loved the way a chameleon changes colors. This book will help those who are afraid to drop their personal masks out of fear of losing a significant other. This book will heal those who find themselves paralyzed with relationship fears. Barbara helps us pose the questions of whether we are standing in our own flame of personal integrity or dancing outside the fire in pain and despair. It takes great courage to be who you really are. Isn't it time that you gave yourself the gift of personal honesty and self love?"

—Carolyn Ann O'Riley, author of *The Remembrance of I AM, An Inner Journey of Self Discovery, A Channeled Course from Archangel Michael*

"With simplicity and truth born from the love that flows from The One within her own heart, Barbara Rose once more reaches out to touch and inspire the hearts and souls of humanity in her wonderful new book."

—Mary Hession, author of *Divine Inspirations*

"With this book Barbara Rose does a great service for humanity, doing nothing less than enlightening the world on the subject of relationships. In addition to reading her work, I've also gotten to know her enough to say that she doesn't just write these things, she lives them. This book is a great gift to the world."

—Gary Renard, best-selling author of *The Disappearance of the Universe*

STOP BEING THE STRING ALONG:

A RELATIONSHIP GUIDE TO BEING THE ONE

BARBARA ROSE

THE ROSE GROUP

Uplifting Humanity One Book at a Time™

STOP BEING THE STRING ALONG:
A RELATIONSHIP GUIDE TO BEING THE ONE

Published by The Rose Group
Uplifting Humanity One Book at a Time™
Florida, USA
www.borntoinspire.com
www.rosegrouppublishing.com

ISBN: 0-9741457-4-2
ISBN: 978-0-9741457-4-7

1. Relationships 2. Self Help 3. Spiritual Relationships

Printed in the United States
Interior design and layout by Words Plus Design

TABLE OF CONTENTS

PREFACE

I decided to write this book after three decades of living in String Along Valley, that place where hopes and expectations from relationships never panned out the way I dreamed they would.

I saw many other people, women especially, who were also playing out their sagas of hoping, waiting, wanting, giving, praying, crying—and ending up in the same String Along Valley.

This valley carries many lessons from rivers of tears shed by all the women who were in love but, no matter what they did or how hard they tried, were left crying and alone.

Much is exposed in this book to get you to see who you are, what a string along relationship looks like—for married as well as single people—and how you can transform yourself from being the String Along to being The One that you really are.

So let's take a walk into this valley. I want you to see the warning signs that will prevent you from falling into emotional quicksand, learn how to move out once you recognize the warning signs, and know what to do once you've decided to soar again.

Whether you've had a string of failed relationships, are currently in a relationship that makes you feel far less than pleased, are male or female—if you want to authentically empower yourself to finally get it right, this book is for you.

I dedicate this book to the One and Only You.

1   STRING ALONG VALLEY

Give me ten minutes and I can tell you if you are destined to being a string along or The One for the rest of your life.

If you think the way The One thinks and do what The One does, chances are you'll be The One.

Falling into the potholes of String Along Valley is far too common in relationships. You can be dating, engaged, living with someone, or married, and still be in String Along Valley.

This is one of the most heartrending and gut-wrenching places on earth. String Along Valley is a place where you subconsciously allow yourself to be strung along in a relationship in which you receive far less than you give.

The valley is filled with anticipation, fear, doubt, anxiety, loneliness, and teases of highs followed by deep lows.

String Along Valley is a place where you walk on eggshells so that you don't rock the boat. It's a place I have been for four years, and a place I will never return to again.

Through the pages in this book, you will see the subconscious string-along messages and behaviors you can easily uproot once you know what they are. And then you can be The One, permanently.

Because I am a heterosexual woman, that's the only perspective from which I can write this book. But anyone, male or female, with any sexual preference, can apply what you are about to learn.

We all have hearts. We all fall in love. We all flip over someone. And I would wager to say we have all had our hearts broken as well.

So let's get down to the nitty-gritty of String Along Valley, and if you see yourself in these pages, just know that I have been through much of this as well—so you have a friend, a friend who will guide you about what to expect, what to watch out for, when to stick it out, when to hit the road leaving skid marks, and how to fully embrace yourself as The One, because that is what you are.

THE DATING GAME

A string along is usually not taken on an official date. (Yes, you can have a relationship and be a string along as well, but this is covered in another chapter.)

During the initial stages of a relationship, whether you call him or he calls you to "come over and hang out" or "stop by when you have the chance," or whether you're called at the last minute, like at 10:00 p.m. on a Friday night or 3:00 a.m. on a Saturday morning—you will be strung along from this moment on.

No true effort was put into treating you as The One. A last minute phone call to conveniently fill a void in someone's lonely night is your first string-along warning sign.

It really doesn't matter how much chemistry you have or how easily you can talk to each other. What matters most is that you were not treated with the dignity and respect of being asked out in advance. Therefore, it's time to hightail it out of this string-along relationship before you get in deeper.

Here are some other verbal string-along warning signs. When you hear them right from the starting line, run—and fast!

THE STRING ALONG EXCUSES

- "I'm married, but we're miserable and I'm going to leave."
- "I'm not interested in getting involved in a relationship."
- "I don't like to talk about feelings."
- "Sharing feelings is too emotional"
- "I make the rules; you follow them."
- "You'll see me on my timetable."
- "I don't like to make dates or plans in advance."
- "I'm not interested in a serious relationship."

- "No pets, no plants, no commitments."

- "I don't have a heart."

- "You might not see me for a few months, so don't expect anything."

- "I never send flowers."

- "I'll sleep with you, but I'm not getting involved."

When people openly express how unavailable they are right from the beginning, listen! They are letting you know in no uncertain terms that they are not looking for a genuine, healthy, authentic relationship.

When we hear those warning signs, we are tempted to fall prey to subconscious [read *"I'll fix this, it won't take that long"*] excuses, and they kick into high gear. Here are the string along excuses we tell ourselves.

- "She's just being self-protective."

- "I should give him a chance."

- "But we just clicked like white on rice."

- "We feel so perfect together."

- "He just needs a lot of love."

- "Maybe nobody else could melt that heart, but I can!"

- "Wait until you have sex with me; you'll change your mind!"

Many of us subconsciously believe that we can actually fix or change another person. We buy into our superhuman subconscious belief that our love will change everything.

When we buy into those beliefs, we place ourselves in the middle of String Along Valley, and we are in for an emotional ride as we try to rescue, save, fix, heal, or love another person—to our own detriment.

Some people can be super charming, and super string-along candidates at the same time. People who don't want to or don't know how to be authentic in a relationship can be pretty tricky while they swoon us with their charm.

Sure, they all know how to put on the charm and lay it on thick when they're just looking to satisfy themselves sexually. They'll say anything. They'll be intellectual, fun, and charming. And if there's chemistry—watch out, baby, because you're about to get burned.

But no, you don't listen to what your smart [read *red flag wisdom*] mind is telling you. You go with your "I can make this better" heart—and you have just entered String Along Valley.

No First Date = No Dating Expectations

If you've met and flipped over the person, and no real first date follows, you're sliding fast. If you've flipped over him so much that you'll go running to him whenever he calls, he knows he doesn't even have to ask you out on a real date. Or you might even anticipate that "he might call tonight to see me," so you take a bath, get dressed like a Barbie doll prop, and wait by the phone. Oh! It rang! Wow! Congratulations. You have just entered blow-up-doll-comes-alive territory.

"Blow-up doll comes alive" is synonymous with "this person is my universe, and I will run and cancel everything just to be with him."

Did it ever occur to you that you deserve a real date, with an advance invitation? When you have a life and high self-esteem, you would never tolerate such treatment. Once you allow yourself to be treated like anything less than The One, you have instantly transformed yourself into the String Along.

You can't blame the guy (or the girl). You can only take responsibility for the standards that you will accept in a relationship. Standards? Yes, that list I hope you will incorporate into your life from this moment forward so that you will never again be treated like anything less than The One.

What standards or qualities would you want the special person in your life to have? Make your own list, and do not compromise on a single thing. You need to know exactly what you prefer and deserve in a relationship. To give you an idea of what you might prefer in a partner, here are some examples of qualities: affectionate, caring, generous, feisty, adventurous, honest, emotionally open, respectful of your feelings, supportive of your life goals and purpose, passionate in bed, ethical, diplomatic, dependable, loyal, creative, sober, drug free, fun loving, intellectual, and down to earth. You might also want someone who has high self-esteem and integrity, listens and communicates well, treats you as an equal, has no addictions, enjoys a sense of humor, is a humanitarian, shares your spiritual values, and follows through on his word.

It's time that you honored your truth in regard to the kind of person you choose to share your time or life with. When you are true to yourself, your relationship will bring you the most joy.

Here are a few good rules of thumb that will keep you on course as The One that you are.

STANDARDS OF THE ONE

First, get to know him before you get into bed, on the couch, or on the floor with him. Give yourself a month to see how this person treats you before you give yourself away.

I'm going to elaborate on this one. Wouldn't you rather get to know someone slowly before spreading your legs? Wouldn't you rather have meaningful sex instead of being just a lay for the night or the weekend? Wouldn't you prefer to know that you are going to be treated well before you make love to someone? That's what trips so many people up. Passionate sex can create a false sense of intimacy in the early stages of a relationship before you even know what this person is all about. It is vital that you protect yourself from falling in too deep and flipping out over someone prematurely before you know more about him.

The One is never a "good time girl." Let him wait a month while you honestly and soberly get to know each other and find out if you have a real connection before you jump into the sack and loose all logical perspective. If the person is just looking to get laid, let him look elsewhere.

You are not the lay.

Sex is not the foundation of a relationship. But you can bet anything that if the sex is great, God help you, because "hot and heavy fizzles out fast."

The foundation of a real relationship is trust, honesty, integrity, and authentic communication. Really seeing what the person is all about. Watching his actions. Does he call when he says he will? Or is it a living hell with no expectations?

You decide what you truly prefer, and go with that.

Second, you will be spoken to only with respect. At the first sign of verbal cutdowns, insults, degradation of any type—hit the accelerator and get out before you lose yourself.

No Show = No You

In other words, if you get stood up, that is the end. The only exception is if he's actually hooked up to oxygen tubes in an intensive care unit.

Zero tolerance for zero follow through

When he says he's going to do something but he doesn't do it, he doesn't want you to count on him. Do you really want to be with someone you can't count on? Who does? It sucks when people break their promises, and it sucks even more if you keep letting it go, forgiving and being let down time after time. That is the only thing that is going to happen. He is showing you that you can't count on him. So bye-bye!

Only date single and available men

I will share two true stories with you to prove this point. When I was fourteen, a woman I'd known for years was in her early thirties. She met a married man. She fell in love. They had an affair. I watched her sad saga play out for more than twenty years. His "business meetings" out of town were their vacations together in the Caribbean. On New Year's Eve she stayed home and cried while he was with his wife. Then there were the promises that he'd leave his wife and the excuses that got more pathetic year after year when he didn't leave her: He couldn't leave his wife until after the holidays. He would leave his wife after his daughter graduated from middle school. He would leave his wife after his daughter graduated from high school. He would leave his wife after his daughter graduated from college. He would leave his wife after his first grandchild was born.

The woman spent two decades of her life in String Along Valley.

Another woman I knew also fell in love with a married man. They had an affair. He left his wife, married my friend, had four children, and then left her for another woman he was having an affair with.

If a man is a cheat and shows no integrity or honesty with the woman he is currently with, how can you expect him to have any with you?

The One never even approaches a married, engaged, or otherwise unavailable man.

You're too smart for that. You're The One.

The One must be treated with respect in public

If someone is going to publicly humiliate you or be rude to you in front of other people, then you can be sure this person has very low self-esteem and is not capable of treating you with decency and respect in private either. Get out at the first sign of humiliation. You deserve much better.

WHAT THE ONE WILL NEVER DO AGAIN

Call and chase after him. It's perfectly okay to take a call, make a call to make plans, and return a call to confirm plans. This is far different from calling several times a day and becoming obsessed and consumed with the other person.

Wait by the phone. You have a life. You can be courteous and return a call when you are able to.

Go over as a last minute get-together. Do not make "last minute" plans the norm from the onset of the relationship. After you've seen the person many times, it's okay to be spontaneous, but because you have a life outside of this person, you need to make plans that fit into your schedule.

Go over as a Booty Call. If you think a last minute lay is going to get you anywhere, I can assure you it will not.

Do a beer run to his place. You are not a delivery service. If you have pre-set plans and you want to bring something over, that's appropriate and kind. But you cannot be there at someone's beck and call. If the person is ill and asks you to get something from the store, that's far different from being on call as a convenience.

Sleep with him within the first month. Become genuine friends. Really get to know the person; then have meaningful sex.

Do his laundry. You are not a laundry service. Unless he has severe physical challenges, he can do his own laundry or pay someone else to do it for him.

Cat or dog sit while he's away on vacation. Hello! You should be with him on the vacation, and the neighborhood veterinarian can take care of the pets.

Cook him dinner or bake him cookies. Unless you have plans to cook a great meal together, save your culinary skills until you really know what this person is all about and if he meets your standards. Your cooking is not going to win him over.

Take any verbal degradation or physical abuse. At the first sign of any verbal or physical abuse, run for your life, and never look back. It will not change. It will only get worse. Do not continue any interaction with anyone who lashes out verbally or with any shoving, pushing, slapping, or hitting. You are not here to be psychologically or physically degraded. You are here to be adored while you adore the person who adores you and shows it in every way.

Many people who are already in relationships are being strung along in misery. Let's take a look at what goes on in a string-along relationship.

2

MIXED MESSAGES

*L*et's say you've known someone for a while. You've been intimate, had sex, had dates or get togethers, and you are treated beautifully when you are alone, but he never invites you out for a date on the weekend.

This is a clear indication that he is playing the field. It means that you get together only on his terms, when it suits him, at his convenience. You don't know where you stand, but because you seem to communicate so well with him, you haven't a clue about what to do.

How can two people get along so well and still have such inconsistency in their relationship? The answer is that Mr. Convenience is keeping you on the back burner, and you allow yourself to be strung along "because you love him."

It's the greatest thing in the world to be there for someone you love—but only if he is there for you in return.

WHAT TO DO WHEN YOU DON'T KNOW WHAT HE'S GOING TO DO

Whether you know what he's going to do or not, you need to set your own expectations—for yourself and for him. Here is what you do not do:

You do not complain.

You do not nag.

You do not demand more of his time than he freely wants to give you.

You do not leave untold hours of your schedule free "just in case" he calls.

You do not cancel plans you have with friends or ignore your other responsibilities when he does call.

You do not ask him, "What is going on?" His actions should tell you what's going on. If he's not being consistent and isn't treating you as The One, then it's time for you to open up your mind and heart and allow someone else to enter.

You do not act rude or uncaring when he does call. Be kind! Be sweet! Be yourself!

The One never plays games. Don't put on an act or act as if you're indifferent. Treat him just as you would anyone else you have a friendship with. And at the same time, do not settle for less than you deserve. Go out on dates. Go out with friends. Read a book. Write a book. Get your life focused on yourself so that you don't revolve your life around him. You are the center of your universe. He is a part of your life. The sun rises and sets over your life purpose—not over his head.

In other words, know what you deserve and expect out of a relationship. If he is not giving it to you, you can't force him to do so. If he doesn't feel it inside, nothing you do will make him feel it. You cannot play a game to try to manipulate him. It never works.

HONESTY

The One is honest. Honesty means you don't lie and make up stories "just to see how he really feels." You should know how he really feels based on his actions. Never lower yourself to live out a lie because you are searching for the truth. This is self-manipulation, and you are too valuable to be manipulated. You are too ethical to compromise your integrity by saying or doing anything that does not come from a place of pure truth. Why do I bring this up? Because I actually tried this. I was deeply in love with a man who told me to find someone else. So I said, "Okay, I will!" But I really didn't. I made up a story about a fictitious man who had every quality I was looking for, and I told the man I really loved that I was so happy with this other (fictitious) man. All of a sudden, one weekend he called six or eight times, day and night. All of a sudden he wanted me back in his life. I thought my game worked. It did—for about a week, and then the man I loved went right back to his old unavailable patterns, and I kept myself in String Along Valley.

It simply was not worth it. I was crying and miserable during my "happy act game," and I was crying and miserable when I continued to receive mixed messages after I thought I got to the truth.

The truth was that I was involved with someone who did not want to be involved. It took a long time for me to develop enough self-love so that I could cut the ties with him completely.

Bottom line: If you have to play games to find out the truth—leave the relationship.

THE MAKE-UP, BREAK-UP CYCLE

Some people, many people, have deep-rooted issues to heal and resolve before they are genuinely capable of being in a real relationship. There is no reason to judge people or put them down if they simply have a lot of healing to do.

At the same time, there is no reason in this universe to drag yourself through the living hell of repeated breakups with the same person. You have to let the relationship go.

If a person says he wants to cut ties, part ways, move on, or say goodbye only to return with a phone call or e-mail days, weeks, or months later, then in his own mind and heart he is not crystal clear about what he truly wants. So what happens to you when you go through many breakups and make-ups?

You are living an emotional nightmare! I know because I lived it. For four years. I kept hanging in there because I thought I really loved him. What about me? What about you?

No matter how deeply you love someone, if the relationship makes you feel as if you're riding a rollercoaster in a nightmare, then you must do everything in your power to get off so you can live with sanity, joy, and inner peace. Breakups hurt, a lot. But trying to ride out a bad relationship just to avoid the pain of a breakup is futile. The only relationship to ride out is one in which the other person is genuinely committed to you and wants to truly work things out with you. But the repeated make-up, break-up cycle is emotional and psychological abuse. This is one of the most difficult and important patterns to break. Only by breaking this pattern will you find the kind of relationship you desire and deserve.

THE "I CAN FIX HIM" MYTH

If you believe that you can fix him, then you believe a myth. Nobody can fix anybody else or change anybody else. You can't change another person's character or behavior or emotions. People who have deep-rooted issues have to take personal responsibility to seek psychological help so that they can heal their own issues. You can't play therapist in a relationship. You are not here to heal anyone else. You are here to heal and uproot your own issues. The person you love may very well mirror and bring your issues to the surface so that you can heal them. But you cannot fix someone else. And the more you try, the more you just string yourself along.

THE "JUST FRIENDS" SCENARIO

In the beginning of a relationship, "just friends" is exactly what you want to be. Before having sex, you want to develop a friendship, find out if you are compatible, and see if you want to go further out of conscious choice. You go out on dates and you talk. This is a crucial time. It's when you learn who the other person is, what he values, what he wants, and how he behaves with you. Everything you learn about him in the beginning, when you're purposely just friends, will greatly help you to make wise choices.

But then, after you've spent weekends together, made passionate sex, talked for hundreds of hours on the phone, and think you know every facet of each other—then he announces that he wants to be "just [read *platonic*] friends."

Mr. Just Friends has just put you in String Along Valley.

After he's spent countless weekends in bed with you, maybe he says he's not ready to settle down or says he's not ready to get serious with anyone What he is really saying is, "Stay in String Along Valley and be there for me while I look around to see if there's anyone better out there for me. You're really great, but I'm not sure. So let me string you along, guilt free,—because now we're just friends. And if I ever decide I want to settle down—well, it's a toss of the dice."

Being in String Along Valley hurts.

If you've been intimate many times, and then he wants to be just friends while you still love him—don't. Get out of the relationship.

A man I know has "just friends" all over the USA. He has great phone conversations with his "just friends," occasional visits, zero commitments, and plenty of other people dangling on the other end of the phone line in String Along Valley who really want to be with him. They are all on the back burner. They are all there to fill his lonely nights— over the phone. And he feels justified because there is no commitment whatsoever.

When you've been holding each other all night long and suddenly you find yourself sleeping on the couch one evening, it's time to go back home and start picking up the phone when another great guy calls you.

Don't string yourself along on the back burner—because when you do, you cheat yourself out of the real thing. If you ever told someone that you wanted to be "just friends" and you really meant it—you know that the relationship is pretty much over.

When you've had passion worthy of an epic novel and then you have no sex, it means you are deep in back burner territory. The more you try to stick it out or ride it through to prove how loyal, caring, lovable, generous, devoted, and sincere you are, the more you burn yourself.

You deserve center stage in a relationship. "Just friends" is for people with zero physical chemistry, people who have never been intimate with each other, people who are not physically attracted to each other at all during the course of a relationship. Trying to be just friends with someone you love, someone you love making love to, is torturous.

Wanting to be just friends can be a control issue by a person who does not feel comfortable with true intimacy. You're not a healer, and you can't heal another person's intimacy issues. On the other hand, it may be that the person has lost romantic interest but does enjoy your conversation. If you still love someone who is no longer romantically interested in you, then the only thing you can do to save your sanity and to spare yourself from countless nights of crying yourself to sleep is to end the relationship. Now.

Allowing and even choosing to keep yourself strung along gives you no chance to be The One, no chance to have it all with someone who really cares about you.

You must be brutally honest with yourself. Do you love him? Do you love sleeping with him, being with him, laughing with him, playing, dancing—are you really into this guy? And despite the way you feel, is he giving you the "just friends" line? Then it's time you honored your truth. As hard as it might be, you must walk away completely. I'll make one thing extremely clear for you. When a man loves a woman, he knows how to go after her. If you were on a rice field in China, he would find you.

Nothing stops true, mutual love.

So if you have been put in String Along Valley, you must get out completely and say goodbye. If you were wrong, he'll find you.

HOW TO MOVE ON WHEN YOU STILL LOVE SOMEONE

So you still love him, but you know you have to move on. How can you do that? Look at the situation honestly, the way it really is now. Don't hope or fantasize about the potential of what the relationship could be "if only." There is no "if only." It was what it was. You each did the best job you could at the time with the level of growth you each had at the time. You can't redo the past. You can only go forward, with gratitude for whatever you learned, and wish the other person well from your heart. Then take a lot of deep breaths and move forward with your life. If something is meant to be, it will be. You have to reach a certain level of trust in your life to know that there is a timing and a higher reason for everything that happens. Maybe you'll get together again in the future. Maybe you'll meet someone else who is everything you have ever wanted. Maybe you could really use some time off for yourself—time to soar and take your life in the most positive direction possible.

Moving forward in your life is what you should be doing anyway, no matter who is in or out of your life. Doing so will keep you focused, positive, productive, and genuine. It will spare you from sleepless nights with tears streaming down your pillow. The One knows she is here on this earth for a very important reason: to focus on her life purpose. This is truly empowering. When you are centered in yourself, passionately filling your days and evenings with everything you want to create to make your own unique difference in this world, then you have "back-up" by you. Then you can be authentic with a man and really live by the standards you have set for yourself, standards that you will not compromise for anyone, ever.

To Recap:

- Be "just friends" only if that is what you truly want.

- Never be "just friends" to string yourself along.

3

LIFTING YOURSELF OUT
OF THE VALLEY
OF MISERY

I know how painful it is to be in love with someone and to keep myself strung along. I cried for countless nights because I allowed myself to be played like a yo-yo. One week it was bliss, the next week no date, nothing. It was a difficult growth experience, but I learned so much as I went through a deep inner transformation. I moved from having low self-worth, and low expectations to genuinely feeling my worth and choosing to move into what felt true for me.

The process I am about to share with you explains how to pull yourself out of the valley of misery when you are in love but are not receiving the full, authentic relationship you deserve in return.

Release all blame. Stop focusing on the flaws and weaknesses of the other person because it drains your focus away from your own life-enhancing growth and experiences.

View the other person with understanding and compassion. Once you really understand that his issues truly have nothing to do with you, once you stop taking his behavior so personally, you will begin to see that his style and level of commitment is all about him and not about you.

Shift your focus to creating what you enjoy. Begin a new day with a commitment to yourself to shine and create the best life imaginable.

Allow your feelings to come up. Simply acknowledge them without judgment. Just notice your feelings. Then, shift your focus to something that is going to make your life better. Do not swim in the emotional ocean of past memories or hopes for the future. Pull yourself fully into the now—because this moment is the most empowering, authentic, and truthful place you can be.

Make a list of everything you want to create in your life. The list will give you a renewed feeling of personal joy and authentic empowerment.

Make a list of every quality you prefer in a potential partner, and stick to your list.

Make a list of every warning sign that tells you to leave the relationship, at any stage—permanently.

For example, I will not tolerate a relationship with a man who uses drugs, is an active alcoholic, is physically or verbally abusive, or is a gambling addict. Those are things I look out for, and at the first sign of any of them, the relationship is over. Other things are on my list as well, all written with my mind and heart. I know what I want and what I will never tolerate. Some people love to gamble and want someone to go to casinos with them. If that's your personal preference, fine. Your list has to reflect your truth—not mine. My list is for me, and your list is for you.

Once you are extremely clear in your heart and mind about exactly what you prefer and will never tolerate, it becomes quite simple to leave when the red flags on your list appear in the relationship.

ADDRESSING FEARS OF ENDING A RELATIONSHIP

Some people remain in a miserable relationship filled with drama, pain, stagnation, and disempowerment out of fear of being alone, erroneously thinking that they will never attract another person or that they will never share a mutually loving and satisfying relationship. Perhaps you think the person in your life is the only one you will ever experience love with.

When you place someone on "the only" pedestal, you falsely buy into the idea that you will never attract another person who will allow you to experience greater joy than what you are currently experiencing.

The one and only is you, not someone else. You can meet and love another person dearly, and should anything ever happen to that person or that relationship, you can love still another person fully and receive love fully as well.

We love many people during our lives. We have different connections to different people. Place all human beings on equal footing with the rest of the human race, and this takes away the belief that you couldn't live without any particular person. This is a false and disempowering belief that keeps people stuck in relationships long after the joy has become a distant memory.

It takes great self-love and inner truth to end a relationship that is barely half as satisfying as one you could create with another, more suitable person.

Here's a saying you may not have heard before: "Know yourself and you know all you are. Disown yourself and you disown all you are capable of."

This saying was created for you from Divine Source so that you will know how important it is to know yourself and to stop compromising yourself for another person when that compromise puts you into misery.

Remember that all emotions flow. At times you may be ecstatic or furiously angry or lonely and sad. Those emotions transform and pass. All feelings do. Not one feeling lasts for eternity. So if you feel sad, know that as you focus on life-enhancing projects and purpose, you will feel a stronger sense of self, and that sense will carry you through the difficult emotional periods.

IGNITING YOUR PASSION AND PURPOSE

What got me to truly feel like The One and have the most solid sense of self-worth was becoming so passionately absorbed in my work—which is my bliss and joy. Find something that you really love to do, and that will help you overcome the deep grief and emotional turmoil of ending a relationship that is in String Along Valley.

WHO YOU ARE FROM THE INSIDE OUT

The only thing that can ever make you feel like The One is realizing how special and important your contributions are, from the inside out, and never again validating yourself from the outside in.

That is the key. What your house looks like, or your car or your bank balance makes no difference. Your position in society doesn't matter. The only thing that matters is who you are on the inside. The One knows she is the one from the inside out.

I have seen women who were dirt poor and overweight, and yet they had the highest self-esteem and self-value. They are incredible women from the inside out. And they had men in their lives who absolutely adored them. Being The One is all about what is on the inside and not what is on the outside.

Some people get sick or have accidents and lose physical abilities—but they are still The One. Some people look like glamour queens, have every material thing they want on the outside, and feel so vacant on the inside. Others pick up on this. Self-confidence and a sense of self-worth can never be faked, and they can never come from the outside in. So if you have been trying to "get" a man (or a woman) by using all of your outer accumulation or looks, then it's time you really made an about face and turned within. It's time to focus on the gem that you are on the inside. If you have difficulty with self-love, make a list of every admirable quality that you do have on the inside. Reinforce and expand your list every day so that you can gain more self-esteem. Stop cutting yourself down completely. Become consciously aware of every time you do put yourself down. When you catch yourself, notice the thought that went through your mind and, without judgment, replace it with a more positive and truthful quality that you do have. Once you do this, you will grow with a lot more self-love and self-value. Then your standards will naturally and authentically rise so high that you will never again allow yourself to settle for anything less than what you deserve. And you deserve the best.

4   Catch Me If You Can

*T*he title of this chapter may sound like a big game, but games and manipulation never work. Instead of trying to catch someone, do an about face; really treasure who you are and consciously decide whether the person meets your standards.

You are the catch—every person is the catch.

Once the games stop and you live a centered, balanced, and authentic life, you would never try to "catch" someone. That is a complete waste of time and energy. The key is to be yourself when you are with someone. If you click with each other, great.

MIXED SIGNALS

When you get mixed signals, you can be sure that the other person either doesn't know what he wants or is trying to string you along.

When a person really wants a sincere relationship, the messages and signals are crystal clear.

So if you are getting mixed signals, back off. Get completely involved in your life and admit to yourself that no matter how you may feel about him, obviously he is indecisive about you. It's time to take a bold step out of String Along Valley.

You don't have to say anything. Your actions will tell the story.

This is not a game. This is facing the truth of the matter. If a man does not want a great relationship with you or wants to play the field and keep you strung along, get out quietly by moving on with your life.

If you whine or ask or nag, he may come up with all kinds of excuses. but he probably will not tell you that he just isn't interested in getting deeper into a relationship with you. That kind of honesty is rare. Or he simply may not want to hurt your feelings. So it takes a lot of guts on your part to look seriously at the messages and signals you are getting and act accordingly—with dignity.

Place yourself in the other person's position. If you really didn't want to get too involved with someone, you know how you would be. You also know that you wouldn't want to hurt him. You may have the integrity to flat out tell him honestly and kindly that you are not interested, but most people avoid confrontations like this, so they communicate through their actions.

Just reverse the situation and don't ever beg anyone to be with you or to give you what you want. It must come from the other person genuinely, because that is the only way you will know if it's for real.

You only want the real thing, not a sorry excuse for a semi-relationship with mixed signals.

Being The One means having the courage to face what is actually happening and having the self-dignity and self-respect to face the truth graciously, without drama and demands.

So if you are receiving mixed messages, it's time to walk away.

WHAT TO SAY IF HE ASKS WHAT'S GOING ON

Now, when you simply get on with your life after having received mixed signals, he will notice. If he asks what's going on, tell the truth. Here's a suggestion for what you can say: "I was getting mixed signals from you, and I know that if I was giving mixed signals to someone else, it would mean that I wasn't too interested in getting involved. So I just noticed what's been happening and let it go."

He may give you more mixed signals or turn on the charm to the highest degree. If you notice a pattern where the "charmer" pulls you in, only to give you mixed signals a few days later, know for sure that you are being strung along—and get out of the relationship.

Mixed signals come from people who are either too afraid to tell you the pure truth, or are so indecisive that they are not capable of behaving honestly. So if this happens, ask yourself one question: Is this what you really want? If the answer is no, then walk out of this string-along relationship so you can open the door for someone else to enter, someone who will give clear messages and communication without all the games. You deserve better. Remember that the longer you keep yourself in string-along territory, the longer you are going to suffer. So get out and shine—because you deserve the best.

5   THE MATING GAME

Some couples date for years and years, without any true commitment. They don't share a home and a life. They may live far away from each other, and continue to date without coming together fully. If this is what you want, if you're happy with this arrangement, then there is nothing wrong with it at all.

But if you would like to share a home with the one you love, and have a life together, after about three or four years it's time to ask yourself if you have been kept in dating String Along Valley.

Unfortunately, your partner may have no intentions of ever coming together fully with you.

He may be content with this "just so far and no farther" relationship. But you need to be brutally honest with yourself and ask yourself if the person you have been perpetually dating shows signs of keeping it that way—permanently.

WARNING SIGNS OF PERPETUAL DATING

- After three years, no ring
- After three years, not sharing a home
- After three years, no actions that show "this is it"
- Broken promises
- Financial excuses
- Living excuses
- All kinds of excuses to not move toward sharing a home and a life.

If you have been in a perpetual, string-along dating relationship and you are not happy, then do yourself a big favor: get out of the relationship so you can have what you truly want. If you are truly happy in the dating relationship, then by all means, enjoy the one you love. The key here is complete self-honesty. Being honest with yourself and acting on those honest feelings will allow you to be happy with the situation in your life.

THE STRING ALONG WIFE

Maybe you're married and your husband treats you like yesterday's newspaper. Maybe your needs are not truly met. Maybe you're the one who puts all of the effort into the relationship only to feel drained and quite unhappy at the end of each day. What do you do? This is your only life. You do have a choice. You can stay miserable, or you can get out. You can try marital counseling to see if you can re-ignite the love and reciprocity you both deserve. If you are miserable and don't do anything about it—do you think that anything will ever change? No, it won't. You can procrastinate for years, staying in a miserable situation, actually stringing yourself along, or you can do something about it. This is your choice—because it is your life. My only suggestion is that you face your truth and let it out. If you don't, sadly, the misery will not change. Remember that you do deserve happiness, without all of the excuses as to why you can't have it. Be true to yourself, and live your truth. Yes, it is scary; but it is also so rewarding.

Give yourself what you deserve—always the best.

TORN BETWEEN TWO LOVERS

Years ago, Olivia Newton-John sang the song "Torn Between Two Lovers." Do you have a lover? Do you have a mate and a lover? Are you living a lie? Are you sneaking behind someone's back? Are you cheating? There is no judgment here. There can be only truth.

I was married to a man who asked me for an open marriage. I had two babies in diapers at the time. I was young and scared. Do you know what I did? I looked at my cheating husband and said, with a lot of laughter: "Do you think I'm going to go out on a date and then come home and sleep in bed with you? Is that the kind of life you think I'm going to live? No thank you—I want a divorce!"

That's exactly what I said, and a few months later, in 1991, I was divorced. There were people who "guided" me to stay with my husband and cheat on him. I was "guided" by people to "have an affair and let my husband support the children and me." I couldn't live a lie. I couldn't do it to myself, and it's the last example I would want to set for my own children. So although it was difficult, I followed my truth, and it was one of the best decisions I have ever made. The truth—your truth—will always be the best decision you can make.

I know women who stayed married and miserable for financial comfort. I don't judge them; I feel sorry for them, because deep inside they are living a lie and denying themselves their truth.

Always remember that when you deny your truth to yourself, misery will remain. When you honor your truth, then you are free to live and be everything you want in this life. It is the most liberating and authentically empowering feeling a person can have.

TILL DEATH DO US PART

Are you married and miserable, petrified to break a vow you made years ago? If you are miserable, there is no judgment or punishment if you follow your truth and free yourself from pain. No matter what any religion or doctrine tells you—ultimately, you must be true to yourself. Never sacrifice your truth because others tell you that you must. This is a controlling lie. And as you well know, "the truth shall set you free." Please remember that.

FINDING THE COURAGE TO LEAVE THE STRING ALONG LIFE

Whether you are single or married, if you are miserable, there comes a time when you have to find the courage to leave.

Here is how to find that courage: Make a clear picture of the new life you want to live. Start working and put money away in a place where only you can access it. Or you may have a dear friend or relative who can hold the money for you if you are in a controlling and miserable situation. Get your cash together, call a mover, and simply move out.

The fear will be there. Or you may be so disgusted that you can't wait to close that door behind you. Just walk out and never look back. Stop making excuses for yourself that keep you in agony.

The only way to change a situation is to change your thoughts about it and then act differently. There simply is no other way. So if you have been living a String Along life, it's time to free yourself.

You have more courage than you know. The fear will subside, but only when you take positive and life-enhancing action will your fears begin to transform into true joy.

You do deserve this—because you are The One.

6

DATING FOR ALL THE WRONG REASONS

*L*et's face it: some people look to relationships for money, clout, social stature, career success, and a mate to have children with. Now there is nothing wrong with having any of those things. But when you date a particular person because you think he can give those things to you, you immediately place yourself in String Along Valley.

You may sacrifice your truth, integrity, genuine desires, and even true love just to obtain those things from another person.

The One knows she can create her joys, passion, success, abundance, and stature (if you feel you really need the stature), and you can even have children without sacrificing your truth.

The term "gold digger" fits quite well here. What are you digging for? There is no need to dig, or get, or maneuver, manipulate, lie, or betray your own truth for anything that is outside of you. The key is to be you.

FROM EXPECTATION TO AUTHENTICITY

Once you realize that you are just as capable as anyone else of creating the life of your dreams, your need for it to come from another person will vanish.

No one can ever give you what exists inside of you—your authentic creative power. But anyone can take away anything they have given you on the outside. Please remember this. I have seen women who thought they had it all, and suddenly, after a break-up or divorce, they lost it all. The one thing that you will never lose is your true sense of self and the enormous power within your mind and heart to create every last thing you have ever wanted to be, express, and experience in this life.

When you look for it to come from someone else, that sends a signal into the depths of your being that you cannot obtain those things for yourself.

The major lesson here is that The One knows who she is, what she stands for, and where she is headed; and she dates out of choice, not out of need. There is a big difference, and that difference affects both how you treat yourself and how you allow yourself to be treated. Never date for what you can get. Always date to share who you really are. Then and only then will you be able to live up to the standards of being The One that you are.

When You Can't be Bought

A relative once said to me, "What you need is a rich old man with a really bad cough." The thought disgusted me. Another day I was standing in the grocery store buying deli for my children. The woman behind the counter asked, "What else can I get for you?" I said, "About ten thousand dollars." I should have known better than to say that; it was just a tight month financially. A man standing beside me said the exact same thing my relative had said years earlier. I turned around, looked at the man with dignity and a smile, and kindly said, "I would never marry for money." He looked a bit surprised, and I walked away feeling like a million bucks.

Bottom line: The One can never be bought. No matter how much people may have, they can lose it all. I've seen this happen to the billionaire family of a student I went to college with in Switzerland. I have seen families have so much and lose it all.

When you have self-respect and high self-esteem, and you can cover the basics completely on your own, you will feel extremely empowered. It doesn't matter what kind of car you drive or what label is on your purse or clothing or lipstick. The only thing that matters is that you choose the person you are going to date, relate to, and love out of authenticity and not out of expectation. You will not date someone to "rescue" you or "make your life better." That is a major no-no for The One.

As The One, even if you live in a one-room apartment, take the bus to work, and eat a lot of vegetables and pasta, at least you are self-sufficient. Nobody can take that away from you. If you are looking for more of the good life, create it yourself. Get excited about creating it from the inside out—and always remember that the outside does not validate who you are. It also does not give you high self-esteem, self-respect, or the guts to walk away when you are being treated like dirt or are miserable in the relationship.

OPTIONS

You know what your standards are with respect to a relationship. You know what your food preferences are when you go on a date and order your meal in a restaurant. The One never has someone make her food choices or any choices for her. The same goes for every aspect of your relationship. You make your choices based on your preferences, and always with a smile.

NO PERMISSION, VALIDATION, OR APPROVAL NEEDED

The One has a mind of his or her own. If you want to make a change in your life, go somewhere, buy something, or do anything, you do not need anyone's permission.

If you are in a situation in which another person has been calling the shots, and you have been going along, even when deep inside you would prefer to do something different, then here is a solution for you.

You can say to the other person: "I hear and understand your opinion, and we're all entitled to our opinions. This is what I want for me, and this is what I am going to do for me because it will make me happy. It's okay if you disagree. I still have to follow my own truth."

That is all you ever need to say. Then do what you really want to do. If the other person gives you a hard time, repeat yourself, and continue to do what you want. In a romantic relationship or marriage, no one else is your ruler, dictator, or boss. Only you can be the boss of your own choices and decisions. So even if accepting decisions made by another person has been a pattern for decades in your life, you must now simply follow your own truth. If your partner screams or creates a dramatic scene, do not buy into it. Follow your truth no matter what. If you feel threatened or afraid, take a good look at your life and ask yourself if this is truly the kind of relationship you prefer.

You do not have to fight or argue; just do what you want to do under the dictates of no one, ever. If you've been controlled for a long time, chances are you will feel petrified to move boldly out of the relationship. And yet, this could be one of the most freeing and authentically empowering things you could ever do for yourself.

The One is not a puppet.

The One calls his or her own shots.

The One is true to self.

The One has the courage to walk when anyone tries to manipulate, intimidate, or control him or her.

The One never lowers his or her own standards to appease another.

The One is not a pushover or a doormat.

The One has a zero tolerance for games and manipulation.

The One has inner strength, self-worth, self-esteem, self-honesty, backbone, courage; he or she is true to self at all times and under all circumstances.

It is when you embrace self honestly that you begin to radiate a glow of authenticity, a glow that will naturally attract a fitting partner into your life. The One never allows another person to have complete decision-making control over his or her life, ever.

HEALING STRING ALONG MISERY

Let's say you've been in a relationship and have spent about 70 percent of it crying in misery. You need to accept that you have not been getting what you desire and deserve from your partner, and plant this seed in your mind: You can have it all with another person.

Once you let go of your chronic and misguided attachment to "the only person on earth you could ever love this much" and replace that attachment with a more truthful perception, you will see that as much as you may love him, you're miserable—and you can live without him just as you managed to do before you met him.

Please remember that if you are miserable and trying to get over a person, you need to remove all of your attention from him and concentrate on your own life instead.

If he has been your life, you have been in String Along Valley, and you deserve to thrive and shine high on your own mountaintop, free from pain and turmoil.

The One never stays miserable for an extended period if the other person is doing nothing to make permanent life-enhancing changes to improve the relationship. You have to make the changes—because sister, no one else is going to make them for you.

The Waiting Game

Maybe you've done what I did when I lived in the mud of String Along Valley. You waited, cried, hoped, imagined, prayed, wished on a billion stars, sent letters, asked, again and again and again for the changes you wanted in the relationship, and it never changed. Stop waiting for an apple tree to give you strawberries! Stop waiting for this person you worship, this person who treats you like a toad, to turn into Prince Charming.

Stop waiting, and start being all that you really are. Be strong, self-reliant, confident, self-sufficient, honest, and dignified. Be kind and sweet when you leave the relationship. Never engage in bitter, ugly behavior. Don't throw his clothes out the window or slash his tires. (I never did this, but

I do know people who have.) Don't lower your dignity—ever. Do not harass, threaten, spread rumors, or speak badly about him behind his back. Just leave him in your past and move on—into the now—and be all that you are for you.

You'll be quite surprised by how quickly you'll get over him once you focus all of your attention onto enhancing your own life and really making a difference in this world. You will be quite amazed at how much energy you will have once you pull your mind's focus from the past into the now. The inner relief will quicken. The turmoil and pain will end. You will smile again, and you won't ever go to places "because he might be there." Ever.

Go to places because you want to be there, and for no other reason.

Begin to create every joy you have ever wanted to experience. Here's a bit of metaphysical and astoundingly true info for you.

Once you begin to radiate into this world all you truly believe yourself to be from the inside out, your energy will radiate as well. As a result, you will attract an incredible counterpart, someone who is much more suitable for you—because you have become aligned with your truth. Have you ever noticed people who seem to have a glowing radiance about them? That is what I am speaking about. The One glows. She knows she is authentic, and cannot be bought; she knows her preferences, who she is, what she believes in; and she never compromises her dignity and truth for anyone.

That is The One that you are.

In the next chapter, you will find guidelines to refer to at different times, just to keep you on track.

7

LOVE, COMPASSION, AND THE COMPLEX RELATIONSHIP

M any relationships are not cut-and-dried or black and white. They fall into a grey area where tremendous compassion and understanding make the difference between being strung along or having the real thing.

WHEN TO STAY

Stay in the relationship if you are both equally committed to making it work, communicating, and creating through your actions the growth and changes you each want in the relationship. As long as you are both doing your best and are committed to having the love of your life in your life, then you can give loving compassion to your partner as well as to yourself.

Suspend all judgment. Replace judgment with understanding. The relationship must be equal and reciprocal on all levels with zero games or manipulation. This is the only way you can have it all; and each of you is The One.

WHEN TO LEAVE

When your relationship is completely off balance—one doing 80 percent of the work, and the other putting in 20 percent when it suits him—then you owe it to yourself to simply leave the relationship with understanding and loving compassion.

Relationships must be fifty-fifty—equal on all levels. You must each give and receive, share, communicate, and honor each other's personal boundaries and preferences. In authentic relationships, there can be no control games that stem from ego. The One never allows himself or herself to be manipulated or controlled.

LOVING AND LEAVING

Love is the most beautiful and wonderful experience on earth. Leaving the person you love is hard, even when that person treats you badly. I just have to ask you one question: Do you love yourself?

You see, self-love does not tolerate an unbalanced, unequal, and nonreciprocal relationship. You are not doing yourself or the other person any favor by settling; if you settle for less than you deserve, you put in motion the dynamic that allows him to also settle for being far less than he is capable of.

You can love someone with all of your heart and still move forward and away if the relationship is not equal, healthy, and reciprocal. Your absence may cause him to do some real soul searching, to ask himself what he truly wants in a relationship.

If you are not receiving what you want in a love relationship, why settle? People tend to fall in love with a person's potential instead of his reality. We all have the potential to grow to become our highest and best selves. As we strip away the layers of ego, the walls, the egoistic responses—we come closer to our authentic Self—and that is what you must be if you truly want to share your life with someone. Additionally, that is what the other person has to be—his or her authentic self. Filled with self-love, compassion, and the desire to create the relationship of his or her dreams with you.

If the one you love is not working on creating the best possible relationship with you, then sad as it may be, it is time for you to move on, with understanding and compassion. Only then will you have all you deserve with someone you truly love.

STRINGING YOURSELF ALONG

If you are stringing yourself along—if you are giving and giving, or taking and taking, in an unbalanced, inauthentic relationship—you'd better either start to do something about it, and fast, or move the person out of your life permanently.

Never settle. Ask yourself how you truly feel in the relationship. Ask yourself if the person you love cares enough to really work things out with you. If the answer is no, then it's time to move out of String Along Valley.

What Is and What "Could" Be

Look at what is now. Go with this and stop fighting what the universe and the other person are showing you. Take a good, clear look at what is actually happening, and accept it as you move forward.

When you linger in "how it could be" territory, you fabricate a mental movie that has nothing to do with reality. As hard as it may be to fully face the reality of your relationship as it is now, you must either do something about it to create the relationship you truly want together or let it go completely with tremendous compassion. Those are your only options.

If you love the person, you can try to make it work. If you can't make it work or if he does not want to make it work with you, then you must say good-bye for your own sanity.

The Yo-Yo Syndrome

You are not a toy; you are not a yo-yo. Either you have the real thing or you do not. Face the truth, and follow what your truth tells you. As long as you avoid the truth of the situation, you will be miserable. But once you really face the truth and take positive action based on complete self-honesty, then you can have the relationship of your dreams with The One you really love.

50 REASONS TO STAY
(YOU NEED ALL OF THEM)

1. You share honest communication.

2. You share similar values.

3. You both have an expressed desire to be in the relationship and to make it flourish.

4. You experience passion in bed.

5. You both follow through on what is said.

6. You respect each other's life path.

7. You respect each other's spiritual values.

8. You support each other in your careers and life purpose.

9. You have a real friendship.

10. You know each other's friends and family.

11. You're available for each other in case of an emergency.

12. You're able to reach mutually agreeable solutions for differing opinions or preferences.

13. You talk out what is bothering you.

14. You acknowledge each other on special days such as birthday and holidays.

15. You can confide in each other.

16. You have a solid sense of self and the courage to speak up when something bothers you.

17. You know where you stand with each other.

18. You work out problems rather than run away from them.

19. You show each other respect in public and in private.

20. You honor and listen to what the other person is trying to communicate.

21. You share similar views on lifestyle.

22. You allow each other time alone.

23. You each allow the other to be who he is and don't try to change him.

24. You each control your own individual finances.

25. You talk openly about changes you see happening in the other person and in yourself.

26. Both of you are single and completely available.

27. You show love, care, and respect to children you may have.

28. You share a vision together for the future.

29. You can work as a team.

30. You can each allow small quirks to go over your head, without a fuss.

31. You can say how you really feel.

32. You both honor and respect the other person's feelings.

33. The relationship has zero verbal, physical and mental abuse—including put-downs and degrading comments.

34. The relationship has zero jealousy, games, and manipulation.

35. You have real dates.

36. After time, you create a full life together.

37. You take short (or long) vacations together.

38. If you live together, you share responsibilities equally.

39. Each of you monitors yourself and not the other person.

40. You both do what you want to do and allow the other person to do the same.

41. You respect each other's exploration of new interests.

42. You know where you stand sexually and are honest with each other about it.

43. If you love each other and are having great difficulties that you want to work out, you seek professional counseling.

44. You are fully supportive of each other's individual expression.

45. You treat each other as The One.

46. You talk to each other rather than to your friends or family about what is bothering you.

47. You do small things for each other out of kindness and love.

48. You let each other know in words and actions that you are there and can be counted on.

49. You take risks by being your authentic self in all areas.

50. You are completely honest, from your heart, and you don't hide your truth because of the fears in your head.

50 REASONS TO LEAVE SKID MARKS
(JUST ONE IS REASON ENOUGH TO RUN FAST!)

1. Either of you is married and not completely available.

2. The other is an active alcoholic or drug user, using substances regularly to avoid feelings.

3. You see the first sign of physical or mental abuse: put downs, degrading comments, pushing, shoving, or hitting.

4. The other person says he does not want to be in a relationship.

5. You are not taken on dates and courted.

6. You are a "friend with benefits."

7. You are called for last minute get-togethers and rarely go out on dates.

8. You're not allowed to express your feelings and are labeled emotional.

9. There is no clear, genuine communication.

10. You feel as if you are walking on eggshells to accommodate the other person.

11. The other person rarely, if ever, lets you know he can be counted on.

12. After six months, you do not know the other person's family or friends.

13. Your relationship is kept secret.

14. After having been physically intimate with you for weeks or months, the other person no longer allows sexual relations.

15. After expressing love for you, he takes back what he said.

16. You rarely go places or do things together.

17. You have vastly different views about life.

18. Your spiritual or religious preferences are not honored and respected.

19. The other person tries to change you.

20. After intimacy, you are treated like a stranger.

21. You are put down in front of other people.

22. You are stood up for a date or plans.

23. Plans are repeatedly broken and not reset for another time.

24. You are sexually abused.

25. He speaks badly behind the backs of other people he is "seeing."

26. Just about every other woman in his life is "just a friend" (that he slept with previously).

27. You are referred to as "someone I know."

28. There is no physical chemistry or passion in bed.

29. You cannot talk to him about anything.

30. If you have a misunderstanding, he ends your relationship rather than talking it out.

31. You never go on any sort of vacation or get-away with him.

32. You are not acknowledged on special occasions and holidays.

33. You are threatened in any manner.

34. Your relationship has all kinds of restrictions and boundaries that prevent intimacy.

35. After a few years you still do not share a life together or a genuine monogamous relationship.

36. He lets you know about the other people he is having sex with (to see if you get jealous).

37. He plays games with your feelings and tries to manipulate you.

38. He cuts off communication when you are trying to discuss something that bothers you.

39. He tells you to find someone else. (Do that!)

40. He can be intimate with you only if he is drunk or high.

41. The relationship is off balance and one-sided, to suit his needs, without reciprocation.

42. Your personal growth is not honored.

43. He tries to control your finances and tells you what you can and cannot spend.

44. You have a telephone or Internet relationship and rarely get together in person.

45. No effort is made to see you in person regularly.

46. He goes out without you and calls you when he gets home in the middle of the night, but he rarely takes you out.

47. He refuses to talk openly about where you stand with each other.

48. He breaks up or stops contact with you repeatedly, and refuses to communicate openly, honestly, and authentically.

49. He makes it clear to you that you are "just friends" after you have been intimate.

50. Weeks go by without hearing from him at all.

Take a good look at both of the lists above. Which one describes your relationship? Do you see it written all over the pages? The second list points to a string along relationship. The One has the first list.

You are The One.

8

GETTING REAL IN A RELATIONSHIP

*U*ltimately, you want a partner you can be your true self with, a partner who will treat you with love and respect.

The subconscious social conditioning we receive to get or capture another causes us to fail and to string ourselves along, while we simultaneously hide our real selves. This robs both people equally of the opportunity to get to know, love, and care for each other, while maintaining a solid sense of self.

BEING EQUALS

It does not matter if you are male or female, nor does it matter what your sexual preferences are. The only thing that matters is that you view yourself and the other person as fully equal human beings.

This means that your preferences and standards are equally as important as the other person's. As a result, they are equally respected.

This means that compromising your integrity or the other person's integrity is not an option.

Games and manipulation are not an option. Do you like it when someone plays games and tries to manipulate you? Of course not. Therefore, trying to manipulate the other person must never even be considered.

Equals do not engage in a power play. There must be mutual respect. You must care enough about the other person's feelings to dare to be honest; and you must be honest even if you feel scared or fear that stating your truth might be hurtful to the other, as long as your motive is pure and comes from your heart.

It is the heart center within each person that ties us all together. Both men and women have feelings, and those feelings deserve to be honored at the expense of no one.

BEING WHO YOU ARE AND TRUE TO YOURSELF

In a relationship, being The One means being who you are, and sharing yourself honestly and genuinely with the other person.

This honesty requires the courage to speak your truth, even if you fear rejection. It means that you stop holding back out of fear and start expressing your feelings kindly and graciously. What matters most is that you express your truth. Holding back your truth out of fear robs you of the ability to share your true self with the other, and it robs the other person of the opportunity to really know who you are, how you feel, what you think, and what you want.

Stifling your truth causes the relationship to break down. It causes the relationship to stagnate or slowly deteriorate. At all stages of a relationship, from the first meeting through decades of being together, sharing your truth will never hurt you. Withholding your truth, however, will always hurt both you and the relationship.

When you share your interests, talents, essence, and life purpose with the other person, he receives the gift of getting to know the incredible being that you are. You must find the courage to show your authentic self; you must risk daring to be the real you.

If you fear loss, ultimately you lose your sense of self. Once you lose your self-worth, you begin to slowly deteriorate. Then, sadly, the relationship naturally follows that same downward spiral. On the flip side, taking a risk to share your genuine feelings, thoughts, and preferences will bring authentic truth into the relationship, and you can both thrive. But if you are not suited for each other, then it is better to part rather than string yourself or the other person along out of any sort of fear.

Don't you want to know the truth about what the other person feels and thinks? Well, the other person deserves to know the same about you.

If you receive a phone call, do not act indifferent, as if you just received a call from a telemarketer. If you are happy to hear from him or her, simply say, "I'm happy to hear from you" or "It's good to hear from you." Say the truth. People want to be liked and appreciated; they don't want to be treated like yesterday's newspaper.

If the other person says or does something that you really do not like, say, "When you said that, I felt hurt" or "When you did that, I felt rejected, and it would be so great if you would have done this instead."

If you let the person know, in the moment, when he does or says something that upsets you, you will simply communicate your truth graciously and, at the same time, let him know what you would prefer instead. You don't need to create a dramatic scene. Simply and calmly state your truth, and show your respect for the other person by letting him know what you would prefer, rather than expecting him to read your mind.

Only you can read your mind. You must communicate clearly so that you can have clarity rather than ambiguity within the relationship. If you're walking on eggshells, promptly stand in your truth and muster up the courage to be real enough to state what is on your mind. This will open the door to clear communication. If the person genuinely wants to be with you, your authenticity will only help by giving him the opportunity to open up and be authentic with you in return.

If your truth leads to a breakup, wouldn't you rather have someone in your life who really wants to be with you? Do you really prefer to walk on eggshells, putting up with words and behaviors that are far less than what you deserve?

This is your choice. You can choose to string yourself or the other along, but in the end, this choice only diminishes your self-esteem.

The greatest way to enhance your self-esteem is to be true to yourself on all levels of your life. This will naturally be reflected in how truthful you are with the other person. Whether you stay together or not, at least your relationship will be authentic. It's always much better to go with the truth in your heart and soul. You can never go wrong with the truth.

TAKING THE GAMES OUT OF RELATIONSHIPS

People don't want to be with others who are pining away for them, willing to sacrifice their truth, integrity, and self-esteem just to go along out of fear of rocking the boat or losing the relationship. Nobody truly wants a doormat.

Neither the person who gets stomped on nor the person who does the stomping enjoys a fulfilling, rewarding relationship that contributes great joy to life.

Nobody wins in a string along relationship. Everybody wins when you are both equally The One.

To attract, thrive, and share a life with The One, to grow together, you have to be The One at all times, with zero games.

Being The One means you do not settle. You refuse to settle because you know your worth. You refuse to manipulate just to get what you want by deception of any kind; you have too much integrity to lower yourself by playing manipulation games. You have too much self-love to sacrifice your truth. You have too much self-honesty to keep quiet out of fear. You care too much for the other as an equal member of the human race to even consider asking him to sacrifice his truth just to please you.

If there are difficulties in the relationship, you must sit down together and share from your hearts everything that is upsetting to you, with each person receiving equal time on center stage to share his feelings, and with a shared desire to come to a mutually agreeable solution.

If you have tried many times to work it out, and you genuinely feel that there is no relationship left that resembles the kind you really desire and deserve, then peacefully walk out of the relationship. Then you can both attract new partners who you can have a mutually satisfying relationship with.

The One doesn't even consider manipulative games or sacrificing self-truth to appease the other, and doesn't keep the status quo out of a martyred sense of self-denial.

View yourself and the other person purely as equal members of the human race. Have a life or create a life that you are passionate about so that you can share who you really are with the other.

Show your real feelings. State your real feelings. If you're not sure of your real feelings, simply say so. If you feel scared, it's okay to say that. This openness creates a platform for authentic intimacy, in which it is safe to share your truth. The other person might very well react with relief because you have the courage to be real instead of hiding behind a façade, pretending to be what you think you're supposed to be in order to gain approval.

The only approval and validation you ever need can come only from within you. Far too many people tiptoe around learned cultural rules and regulations to "capture" the other person. How about being the real you so that the other person has an opportunity to get to know who you are and what you're all about.

You don't have to go overboard to prove how lovable and incredible you are. The key to taking the games out of relationships is to stop playing head games with yourself, trying to figure out how you can "get" or "keep" the other person. The key is in getting and keeping your own life, and seeing the other person as a part of your life rather than your central focus. Don't just pretend to be busy—be passionately absorbed in your life! Don't just say you're not available; be available when you can be, but honor the other priorities in your life. Waiting by the phone is not a priority.

If you focus on the other person as the be-all and end-all of your life purpose, then do yourself a big favor: take that focus and place it on becoming your best self and on contributing your best to this world. Then, when you are genuinely available to see the other person, see him and have a blast. If you feel like sending flowers, send them. If you're in a relationship and you both want it to thrive, it's okay for a woman to do something kind for a guy, and vice versa, as long as kindness is reciprocated. The relationship must be equal on all levels. If it's not, why are you still in it? If you're being taken for granted, leave. If you're being treated the way you have always wanted to be treated, then treat the other person the same way. Take the male-female games out of the equation. Games may work for a short time, but they never make for a healthy, authentic relationship. In the end, games don't work.

If you think you have to put on an act or cover up your true self, then it's time to ask yourself what you are so afraid of. Usually the answer is that you're afraid the real you is not lovable. To counter that, be who you really are.

If you make truth the rule of thumb on all levels, you cannot go wrong. If you need more solitude, simply say so. If you would like to see the other person more, it's okay to say, "I have such an awesome time with you. It would be great if I could see you more." Then, trust your instincts about the response you get. If the other person is swamped, then understand. If you're picking up signals that you sense are nonsense, then honor what your smart intuition is telling you, and get busy with your own life, with zero complaints. Someone can be busy but still call. Someone can be out of town and still send flowers. Someone who really cares shows it. Moreover, when you really care about you, you can show it to yourself by the excitement you put into your own life, and by sharing your activities with the other person when you do get together.

Stop worrying so much if you are "getting it right." Be your shining self.

Stop worrying if you are going to "mess everything up." Be honest.

Stop worrying about who should be chasing whom. Share your authentic self.

Stop settling for less than you deserve. State what you prefer.

Stop compromising your integrity. Deal truthfully with the other person on all levels.

Stop wasting your time trying to capture the other person. Let your life purpose capture you.

Stop being the string along. Honor every feeling you have, and dare to be true to you.

9

ANSWERS TO THE 10 MOST COMMON RELATIONSHIP QUESTIONS

*D*uring the final stage of writing this book, I wanted to make sure all bases were covered. I want you to have a thorough book that you can refer to at any time and in which you'll find real answers. To that end, I asked my newsletter subscribers in more than sixty countries to tell me the one question about relationships they would most like to have answered.

I received an enormous response and selected the most commonly asked questions that apply to men and women equally. I am deeply grateful to my subscribers for the questions. Now here they are, with the answers for you.

QUESTION:

What to do if one person in the marriage grows spiritually and the other stays the same and refuses to acknowledge the other person's beliefs as right for them? My husband thinks that my study of metaphysics is just temporary and that I will come back to his religion. I don't know how to handle this, but the issue involves every aspect of our relationship. I don't feel connected in any sense except by our two small children, aged 4 and 2.

ANSWER:

It is vital that you continue to follow your truth with respect to your spiritual growth. No one has the right to judge, criticize, or coerce you to follow his religious or spiritual preferences. This is not up for debate. You do not have to convince your husband or seek approval from him or from anyone else regarding your personal truth, spiritual values, or beliefs. Quite frankly, it is no one's business but your own.

So I would advise you to ask yourself why you are staying in a relationship when the only connection you feel is through your children. If you feel the relationship is not satisfying and if you feel that your personal and spiritual growth are not being honored, it is perfectly okay to remove yourself from criticism, misery, and condemnation from the man you are sharing your (unhappy) life with.

Alternatively, you can stand in your truth and state that your spiritual growth will never be judged or dictated to by any other human being, and ask your husband to accept you for who you are, despite his differing views. Ask him if he would like it if you tried to dictate his religious preferences. You can ask him to honor who you are, and if he refuses to do so, then you do have the option to end the relationship that is more hurtful than supportive. You deserve respect on all levels. Please remember that.

QUESTION:

After 28 years in a dysfunctional marriage, I finally divorced my husband. That was 14 months ago. Now we are both changing and are back together, realizing that we both needed to change to become healthier people. With God's blessings, hopefully, do you think we can become what we both need for ourselves and for one another?

ANSWER:

Absolutely! This is actually fantastic to hear. When two people love each other and realize that they both need to take personal responsibility to heal and evolve on all levels of personal growth, when each partner is committed to his own personal growth and supportive of his partner's process, this is a gift.

Our greatest growth in relationships comes from being in relationships, not in isolation. Always share honestly. Always be true to self and have the courage to be real with your partner. You can never go wrong.

QUESTION:

How can you use your intuition to figure out where you should move to, to meet your partner, if you are currently single? I am going to move from the town I've been living in for 25 years and want to know how I can figure out where I should move to.

ANSWER:

Dear One, when you move to another town because *you* want to live there, to enhance your own life, and for no other reason, you will attract someone who is living his or her truth as well, rather than searching for a partner. The key here is in *attracting* by living your life for you rather than searching to fill a void. You will find that when you least expect it, someone who mirrors where you are within yourself will pop right into your life. So thrive and create the best life you can. Passionately fill your days and nights with all you love to do, and you will attract someone who is living his or her life that way, someone who will mirror you.

QUESTION:

How will I know when I am truly ready to be in a relationship, after not being in one for over eight years? I quit trying after my last relationship turned out to be just like my ex-husband, who was an alcoholic, used cocaine, and went into violent rages. I was severely abused by my natural father, sexually, emotionally, and physically . . . then sexually molested by my brother, brother-in-law, and stepfather (who also beat us). I know from counseling that my relationships with men were my way of trying to "fix" my father/male role models. I think I'm not ready to be in a relationship yet because I feel that I have nothing to offer. I am 200 lbs. overweight and have no teeth. I am also in severe pain most of the time because of fibromyalgia and lower back pain from a fall several years ago. To lose weight I need to exercise, but I am in so much pain that it's almost impossible. I sometimes feel overwhelmed by all of this and discouraged, but I keep going. I am also an insomniac, and when I do happen to fall asleep, I usually have horrific nightmares. I am telling you all of this not for you to do something about it but so that you will understand my original question about relationships. What is a normal relationship, and how do I know it's love?

ANSWER:

First, know with absolute certainty that you do have a lot to offer, even just by sharing authentically. It took a lot of courage for you to open up, and so many people can relate to you. Many others have asked for similar answers, so I thank you for your question.

Now, it is time you forced yourself to discover every wonderful quality you have from the inside out. Your worth is not determined by your weight or your teeth. All of this can be adjusted. You can get a dental bridge and have teeth. Some people are overweight due to thyroid problems, and they are just as worthy as people who are stick thin. This is a time to love yourself by discovering what you truly love, what you really want to express from within concerning your life purpose. These discoveries will help you to heal your self-degrading feelings. Take heart. I used to be the world's biggest doormat. I had an unhappy childhood, failed relationships, and very low self-esteem. I had to discover my passion, find my value from the inside out, and express it as my joy-filled work each day in order to feel my value as an equal member of the human race.

Nobody is better than you. Nobody is less than you. A normal relationship is one in which you can value yourself and the other person equally. In a normal relationship, you are treated beautifully, and you treat the other person beautifully. A normal relationship has one prerequisite: you must really love yourself. Plenty of people who write to me and many people I know look like models, and they still feel unworthy. I used to be one of them, too.

Ask yourself this: If you had ten million dollars in the bank and could do something for the rest of your life that would fill you with great joy, what would that be? What would bring you so much joy that you would do it for free? Search within for the answer. It will lead you to discover your life purpose. Who are the people you admire and connect with from your heart? What are they doing with their lives? That is a good indicator of a natural direction for you, a natural purpose for your life. Moreover, perhaps you suffered the experiences you have been through so that you could reach out and help others overcome their abuse and pain. Usually, our greatest challenges lead to our greatest life purpose fulfilled.

You do have a special purpose. And you are a special human being. Look into your heart to discover what really matters to you. Then bring it out into your life as your work. Being an example stems from your heart, not from your looks. You will attract a wonderful man into your life once you discover and believe that you are wonderful.

QUESTION:

Is unconditional love possible between two persons in a relationship?

ANSWER:

Yes, as long as they both love themselves unconditionally, without self-judgment, self-criticism, or self-abuse of any kind. You can only give what you have on the inside.

QUESTION:

How can I help myself to recognize the "one" that I am supposed to spend my life with?

ANSWER:

When you can be your authentic self in every way with that person, when you treat each other equally and beautifully, love each other's company, communicate openly and honestly, share similar values, respect each other on all levels without ever compromising your truths, and have wonderful chemistry and passion in bed, then you will recognize that you have found "the one" for you.

QUESTION:

Is there a soul mate for each person?

ANSWER:

Yes, but not every person meets a soul mate in this lifetime. Many people have soul agreements to work out karma from previous lives together or to support each other in this life. We also may experience a soul level recognition with many people in our lives, such as with our best friends or relatives.

A soul mate relationship is not always a bed of roses. It can be one of the most growth-filled and transformative relationships we ever have; and it may or may not last for the remainder of this life, although it serves a deeply important purpose for individual growth.

If you want to attract a wonderful match or spiritual partner, grow to love yourself deeply with genuine appreciation for the person you are. Shine and express all that you came into this life to be and express. You will certainly and naturally attract a wonderful counterpart who will mirror your highest level of growth, and you can share an astounding relationship with that person as your equal on all levels.

There is no "perfect" person. Thinking of a soul mate as such is a myth. But you can attract an incredible person into your life once you become the incredible person you came into this life to be and express on all levels.

QUESTION:

Why must we be prepared to accept that some wonderful relationships, even of soul mates, are destined to end? Phrased differently, how can we know if a sacred contract is going to result in a relationship ending? How can we carry love forward from that point?

ANSWER:

We cannot hold on to another person for dear life. We never know if suddenly a person is going to be out of our lives. The most important thing is to be and share your greatest self with the one you love, and create the most joy-filled life possible each moment you are fortunate to experience love with another. Life is filled with constant change. Love with all of your heart, share all of who you are, do your best, be your best, express your truth, and always allow the other person the same freedom of being and expression. There are no guarantees in life, but loving fully and purely is one of the most rewarding experiences of life on earth.

QUESTION:

How will I ever feel that I can trust enough and become vulnerable enough to be emotionally intimate with someone without giving away my power?

ANSWER:

The only way you can ever trust another is to first trust yourself, your feelings, your instincts—and listen to them. Then a person can earn your trust over time and through many small experiences. Notice what you instinctively pick up on. Watch to see if the person's words and actions match.

Don't just give all of your trust to others without getting to know them over time.

When people show you that they can be counted on by following through on what they say and by sharing themselves, you can slowly open up and share yourself. You can share your truth and be emotionally intimate by standing in your truth, regardless of what they do or say.

Never back out of what is true for you to please another person—*that* is giving away your power.

QUESTION:

How do you change someone's belief system?

ANSWER:

You don't. Ever.

Would you like it if someone tried to change your belief system?

You must respect all human beings enough to allow them to be who they are, even if you have different preferences or beliefs. *You* are not on this earth to change your belief system to please any other person. Therefore, no other person is on this earth to change his or her belief system to please you.

QUESTION:

Sometimes you can be in a dating relationship and it can be great, and then you get a vibe that the partner is not 100 percent there, as they once were. Immediately, women in general start to analyze: "Why didn't he call me? He always calls me at this time. What does that mean?" Then women start to doubt themselves, overanalyze, and wind up making it worse. Women then say: "Well, if he's not calling me, I'm not going to call him." And they start giving out weird vibes and all turns to dust.

When you are feeling doubt in a relationship that once was strong, what do you do? How do you address it?

ANSWER:

The best thing to do is to get super absorbed in your life, your purpose, and allow the other person his or her space.

Then, when you do speak, you can make plans to laugh and have a blast for the next time you get together.

If you are secure within yourself and truly absorbed in your life purpose, you may notice that you don't always have the chance to make a call at the exact same moment every day. But if your world is revolving around the other person's phone call, then of course you're going to feel insecure, because you are more focused on the other person than on yourself.

Sometimes people need some breathing room, time to call their own. Maybe they just want to rest or are on the phone with a friend or are watching a movie and don't realize what time it is. Or maybe they are losing interest. Either way, the more centered you are within your own life and the more centered you feel within self, the less this is going to disturb you. When you do see each other, laugh! Create a great time. Create a wonderful memory. Share what is going on in your life, and show interest in what is going on in their life.

When you have a great deal of self-worth, your life will never hinge on another person. Never make the other your oxygen tube for a happy existence. Make your life purpose and sharing your life with the other a joy rather than an obligation.

When you are together, if the other person is acting distant or different, you can say something like: "I want you to know that I care if there is anything bothering you. And if there's something bothering you with respect to me, I want you to feel safe that you can let me know, no matter what it is, and we can address it honestly with each other."

This lets the person know that you are strong enough and open enough to listen, even if it might be to something you may not want to hear. If they think you're going to crumble, and they are your world, chances are that they will avoid telling you something that they think might crush you. If you let them know that they can talk honestly, and it's all okay, chances are greater that they will share anything that may be bothering them with respect to you. More than anything, be their genuine friend, at *all* stages of a relationship. Then you can each share authentically, with full respect for each other's feelings, and you can clear the air at any time, honestly.

QUESTION:

How do you determine early in a relationship if there is a great chance for success? The reason for my question is this: I have been in a relationship for close to six years, and my significant other decided to break things off. She says it's because she has a fear of commitment. How could I have seen or known this earlier?

ANSWER:

The truth is that we do not know if a relationship is going to last forever. If a person has commitment issues and shows that right from the start, then there is nothing you can do or say to change the other person. Trust me on this. I tried it for four years in String Along Valley. Moreover, if you were with a person and decided that you did not want to continue the relationship or share the rest of your life with her, you would have every right to follow your truth. She simply did what she wanted to do, and by doing so she opened the door for you to attract someone into your life who is looking for all you are.

It's usually a gift when people leave our lives. I learned a saying: "When the universe says no, that means there is a better yes for us on the way!

Next time, you will be able to look over the string along warning signs, and that will help you notice a lot more in the beginning of a relationship that you may not have been aware of previously.

In any relationship, you can only live in the moment. It is in the moment that you can share and express any concerns that you have. Open and honest communication is the absolute key to a successful relationship. That is the way for you to know and see it all truthfully, so that you will know what to do each moment of your life.

10 SACRED RELATIONSHIPS

*T*his chapter was originally written through me from Divine Source and was posted in the "Ask Barbara" section of my Web site, borntoinspire.com, to help people with their spiritual evolution in romantic relationships. I added this divine information to this book because so many people found it to be extremely helpful.

The information leads us upward along the spiritual spiral, looking at spiritually evolved relationships and how the dynamics work when people reach this level of spiritual growth.

Many people are evolving spiritually at an incredibly accelerated rate. Relationships sure look a lot better and more promising from this perspective, which indicates where we are headed as spiritual human beings, passion included.

THE QUESTIONS AND ANSWERS FROM DIVINE SOURCE

1. What is a sacred relationship?

2. How does a sacred relationship differ from the relationships we have had in the past?

3. Why is this change taking place?

4. How can I change my perspective to adjust to this new paradigm?

5. What will happen if I make this adjustment?

6. How are the roles of men and women changing now on the spiritual level?

1. What Is a Sacred Relationship?

A sacred relationship is one in which all of the encoding on the cellular level from the eons of conditioning of humanity is now evolving to catch up to your spiritual evolution.

This means that the roles men and women have played are now coming up to the Light to be readjusted and awakened on all levels.

This is a time of great transition, as the old and outmoded ways of belief and actions are consciously replaced with spiritual harmony, respect, and gender neutral preferences. What I mean by "gender neutral preferences" is that you are to view each other as pure spiritual beings, without all of the games and programming that have not served you well in the history of humanity.

This is a time when "do unto others as you would have them do unto you" plays its greatest role.

There will be more of a shared sense of purpose, a shared spiritual service in whatever form of service you chose to come into this life to express. But in this new relationship paradigm or view, you will no longer have a war between the sexes but will honor each other as equal spiritual beings.

The games of old no longer work, and quite frankly, the reason they never worked is that many of your societies and cultures have conditioned you to react and respond rather than to be pure, transparent, and genuine with all of your intentions.

So in this new relationship view on Earth, you can have more open telepathic communication, more of a "knowing" that does not need words to be expressed, and more of a spiritual intimacy that transcends the purely physical intimacy; however, physical intimacy will continue to be delightful and pleasurable, and even more so as you share purely.

2. How does this sacred relationship differ from the relationships we have had in the past?

Typically, chaos and discord seem to precede newfound clarity and resolution. So you might see an increase in the divorce rate. You may outgrow the one you're with while aligning with your higher purpose, if your partner does not support your spiritual growth.

Many of the relationships you have had in the past seemed to require vows—forever. In this new view, relationships will allow for personal freedom on all levels. Faithfulness will come from a genuine heartfelt desire to be together rather than a legally imposed order, an order that as you may surmise has not really worked in your societies anyway.

As you and your partner awaken on all levels, you will not be able to keep secrets from each other because you will literally be able to read the other person's mind.

So you will experience a special level of intimacy as your genuine desires are both known and respected.

During this transition, it is imperative that you learn how to verbally communicate any negative feelings so that they can be cleared up immediately.

Another difference will be in sexual preferences and desires. Certainly sex will continue to be most pleasurable; however, you may not feel the need for as much physical sex. But when you do have sex, it will be a sacred and spiritual merge, and quite powerful to say the least. The power will come from its purity. The passion will erupt, and you will engage in sacred sexuality that transcends the now typical one-night (empty) stand.

Know that it will be and feel far more powerful and real than what has previously been the norm in your experiences, which will make it that much more delightful. In some cases, you may not feel this need to merge on this more physical level.

When you do engage in it, expect it to be more powerful.

3. Why is this change taking place?

This change is taking place because you are awakening to your spiritual nature. As a result, your physical experiences will evolve and awaken along with your spiritual experiences.

Once you grow and awaken on a certain level, you really cannot go backwards in your evolution or awakening.

All is motivated by pure love.

Being that your essence is pure love, you (as humanity) are awakening to your highest expression of Self, and are more consciously becoming one with Divine Source. Naturally, as you become more conscious or awakened, your physical life and relationships are going to follow suit.

This is a positive awakening, and you did choose to come into this world of form to awaken on all levels, to know that you are not nor could you ever be separated from Divine Source. You will begin to experience more of a pure, unconditional love for all, equally, and transcend the view that your partner is more special than any other spiritual being.

As you awaken to this fact, *all* of your relationships become sacred, because you are all One.

4. How can I change my perspective to adjust to this new paradigm?

You can change your perspective by viewing every single being as if you were viewing yourself. Make no separation between "you" and "them" because there is no separation. The idea of separation is all within the erroneous thought system stemming from ego.

So as you act toward another, first, before any action or non-action, ask yourself just one question: Would I like it if this person behaved this way toward me?"

That is the *only* question you need to ask yourself. This will spare you from much unnecessary discord and confusion, and it will certainly spare you from most of the pain you go through because of the outmoded views lodged within your cellular memory that carried over from lifetime to lifetime.

If you can remember to simply view all people as if they were you, then you will adjust to this new paradigm, and you will find much more inner peace and joy in all of your relations with every sacred spiritual being on Earth.

5. What will happen if I make this adjustment?

If you make this adjustment, you will come to know an inner and outer peace that you may never have experienced before. You will feel a sacred connection to all people, and you will feel the oneness that you share with all of humanity, as you may have felt this shared sense of oneness with just one special person.

Now, you will feel this interaction with all people, and it will bring you a great deal of joy with respect to how you relate to and are treated by others.

Please realize that all others are truly a part of you.

It may take many years to adjust to this new view; however, this is the next step in awakening to your divine heritage while you are still in a physical life.

In truth, you are all One, so now you can play this out on the physical level and marvel at the results that come from love on every level of your life.

6. How are the roles of men and women changing now on the spiritual level?

The roles of men and women are becoming more of a shared spiritual experience. They are beginning to be perceived as spiritual humanity rather than "man and woman."

This is the truth, and as all truth is eternal, you will come to find that as your views begin to evolve and awaken, the war between the sexes will cease.

You will look for common ground in your spiritual heritage that will carry much more meaning than motives based on physical means to the ego's trap of a perceived victory or end—the old ego games consisting of eons of past conditioning to capture another person or to manipulate them just to suit your needs, without caring for their needs and feelings as much as you care for your own.

So you will slowly adjust and actually *love* the awakened way much more than the ways of old that were created by your egos.

As a result, you will feel much more inner peace, and the confusion that used to prevail in relationships will be transformed to a spiritual, sacred, shared experience, which will help you to experience the bliss and joy of home that is within your soul memory.

You will begin to feel at home again while in your physical life, and that feeling is one of *pure bliss,* heart-centered joy, and divine love that will permeate every level of your life.

So as you awaken to this level, naturally the roles of men and women will transform to match your new awakening, and what a joy that will be for you and for all of humanity.

About the Author

*B*arbara Rose is an internationally acclaimed public speaker, spiritual author of *If God Was Like Man*, and *Individual Power: Reclaiming Your Core, Your Truth, and Your Life*, founder of The Rose Group publishing company, *inspire! Magazine*, Institute of Higher Self Communication, and Rose Humanitarian Alliance. She works in Divine Cooperation with others to uplift the spiritual consciousness of humanity. Through a Divine Spiritual gift she brings through information to create the highest vision of your life, and our world. Her internationally praised seminars, widely published articles, Higher Self Certification intensives, and Divinely Channeled private consultations have changed the lives of thousands across the globe.

You can visit Barbara's websites at
www.borntoinspire.com and
www.inspiremagazine.info

CPSIA information can be obtained at www.ICGtesting.com
Printed in the USA
BVOW08s1850061213

338410BV00001B/33/A

9 780974 145747